Go West, Ox!

Written by Jeanne Willis
Illustrated by Woody Fox

Ox sat in a pen.

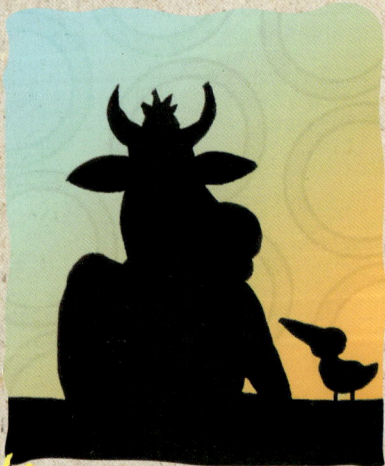

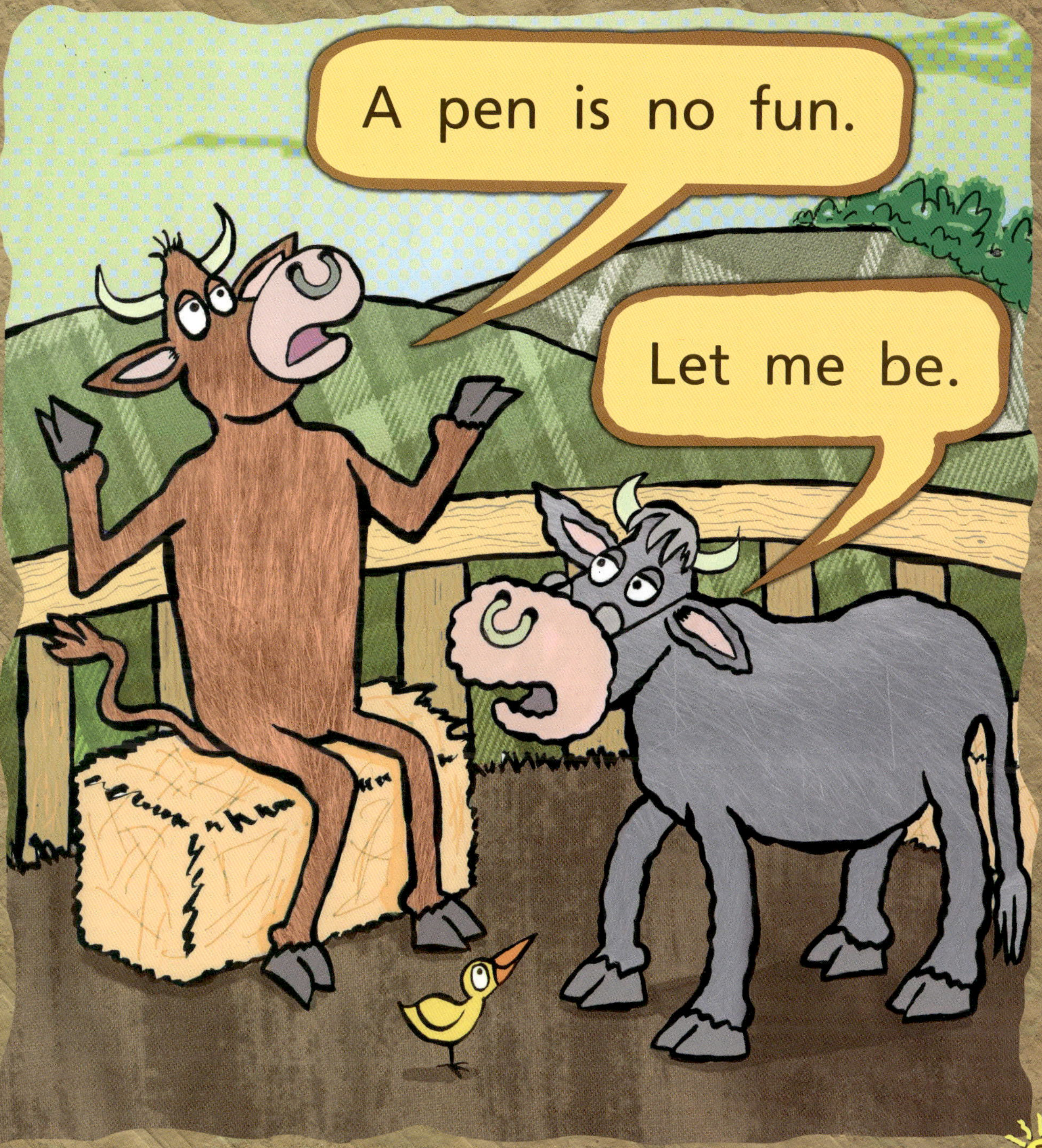
A pen is no fun.
Let me be.

Ox had a plan.

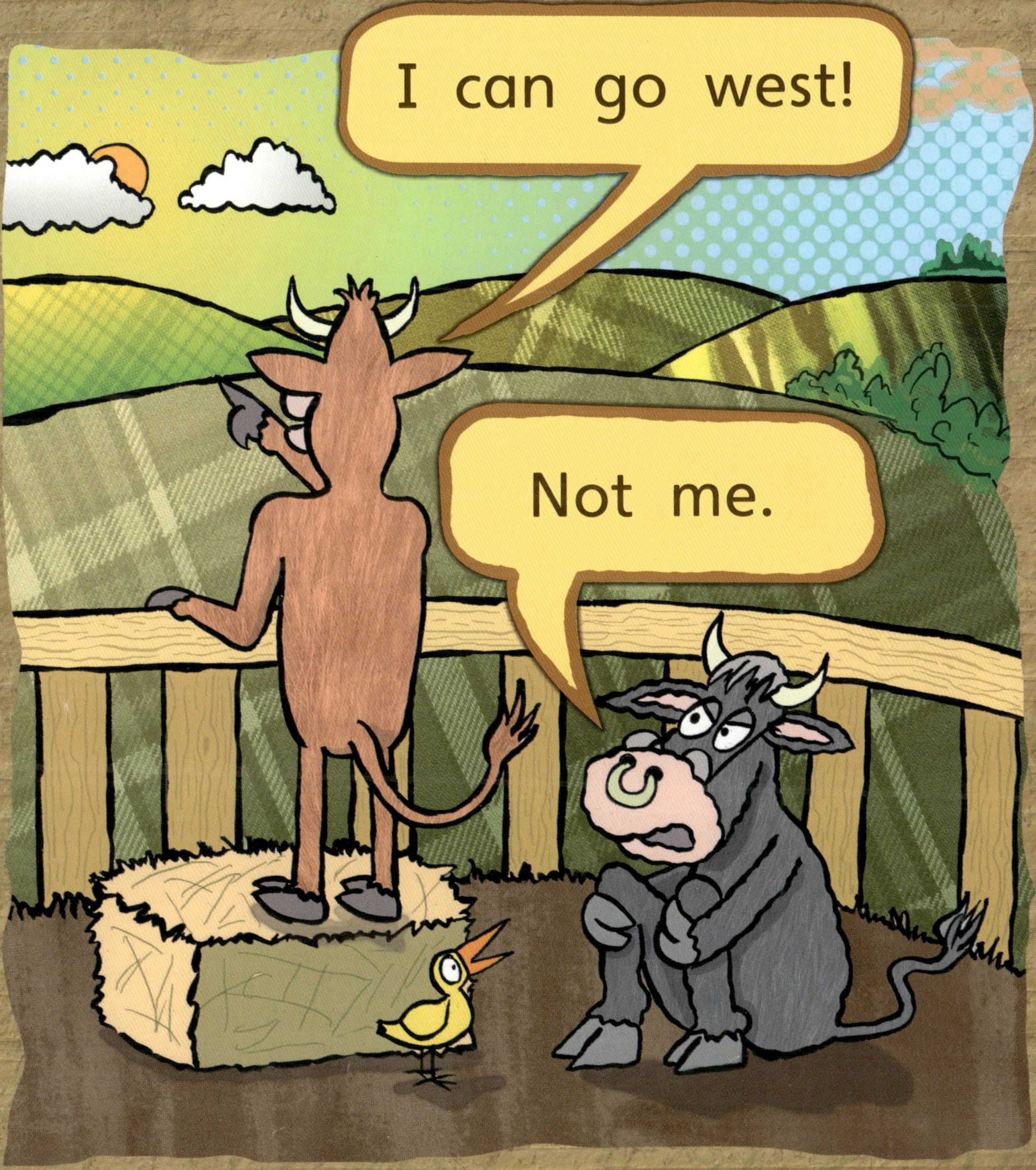
I can go west!
Not me.

I will pack a bag!

Slam!

Ox jumps into a van.

Vvvvvvvvv!

Sat Nav!

But Ox hits a box.

Biff!

9

The van hisses and stops.

No! It is the cops!